D0175219

WHY NOT SOCIALISM?

WHY NOT SOCIALISM?

G. A. Cohen

Princeton University Press

Princeton and Oxford

Published by Princeton University Press, 41 William Street,
Princeton, New Jersey 08540

In the United Kingdom: Princeton University Press,
6 Oxford Street,
Woodstock, Oxfordshire OX20 1TW

Library of Congress Cataloging-in-Publication Data

Cohen, G. A. (Gerald Allan), 1941–
    Why not socialism? / G.A. Cohen.
       p.   cm.
    ISBN 978-0-691-14361-3 (hardcover : alk. paper)
1. Socialism. I. Title.
    HX73.C649 2009
    335—dc22   2009007472

British Library Cataloging-in-Publication Data is available

This book has been composed in Palatino

Printed on acid-free paper. ∞

press.princeton.edu

Printed in the United States of America

10   9   8   7   6   5   4   3   2

CONTENTS

WHY NOT SOCIALISM?

THE QUESTION that forms the title of this short book is not intended rhetorically. I begin by presenting what I believe to be a compelling *preliminary* case for socialism, and I then ask why that case might be thought to be *merely* preliminary, why, that is, it might, in the end, be defeated: I try to see how well the preliminary case stacks up on further reflection.

To summarize more specifically: In Part I, I describe a context, called "the camping trip," in which most people would, I think, strongly favor a socialist form of life over feasible alternatives. Part II specifies two principles, one of equality and one of community, that are realized on the camping trip, and whose realization explains, so I believe, why the camping trip mode of organization is attrac-

1

tive. In Part III, I ask whether those principles also make (society-wide) socialism *desirable*. But I also ask, in Part IV, whether socialism is *feasible*, by discussing difficulties that face the project of promoting socialism's principles not in the mere small, within the confined time and space of a camping trip, but throughout society as a whole, in a permanent way. Part V is a short coda.

I
THE CAMPING TRIP

You and I and a whole bunch of other people go on a camping trip. There is no hierarchy among us; our common aim is that each of us should have a good time, doing, so far as possible, the things that he or she likes best (some of those things we do together; others we do separately). We have facilities with which to carry out our enterprise: we have, for example, pots and pans, oil, coffee, fishing rods, canoes, a soccer ball, decks of cards, and so forth. And, as is usual on camping trips, we avail ourselves of those facilities collectively: even if they are privately owned things, they are under collective control for the duration of the trip, and we have shared understandings about who is going to use them when, and under what circumstances, and why. Somebody fishes, somebody else prepares the food, and another person cooks it. People who hate cooking but enjoy washing up may do all the washing up, and so on. There are plenty of differences, but our mutual understandings, and the spirit of the enterprise, ensure that there are no inequalities to which anyone could mount a principled objection.

It is commonly true on camping trips, and, for that matter, in many other non-massive contexts, that people cooperate within a common concern that, so far as is possible, everybody has a roughly similar opportunity to flourish, and also to relax, on condition that she contributes, appropriately to her capacity, to the flourishing and relaxing of others. In these contexts most people, even most *anti*egalitarians, accept, indeed, take for granted, norms of equality and reciprocity. So deeply do most people take those norms for granted that no one on such trips questions them: to question them would contradict the spirit of the trip.

You could imagine a camping trip where everybody asserts her rights over the pieces of equipment, and the talents, that she brings, and where bargaining proceeds with respect to who is going to pay what to whom to be allowed, for example, to use a knife to peel the potatoes, and how much he is going to charge others for those now-peeled potatoes that he

bought in an unpeeled condition from another camper, and so on. You could base
a camping trip on the principles of market exchange and strictly private ownership of the required facilities.

Now, most people would hate that.
Most people would be more drawn to the
first kind of camping trip than to the second, primarily on grounds of fellowship,
but also, be it noted, on grounds of efficiency. (I have in mind the inordinate
transaction costs that would attend a
market-style camping trip. Too much
time would be spent bargaining, and look-
ing over one's shoulder for more lucra-
tive possibilities.) And this means that
most people are drawn to the socialist
ideal, at least in certain restricted settings.

To reinforce this point, here are some conjectures about how most people would react in various imaginable camping scenarios:

a. Harry loves fishing, and Harry is very good at fishing. Consequently, he catches, and provides, more fish than others do. Harry says: "It's unfair, how we're running things. I should have better fish when we dine. I should have only perch, not the mix of perch and catfish that we've all been having." But his fellow campers say: "Oh, for heaven's sake, Harry, don't be such a shmuck. You sweat and strain no more than the rest of us do. So, you're very good at fishing. We don't begrudge you that special endowment, which is, quite properly, a source of satisfaction to you, but why should we *reward* your good fortune?"

b. Following a three-hour time-off-for-personal-exploration period, an excited Sylvia returns to the campsite and announces: "I've stumbled upon a huge apple tree, full of perfect apples." "Great," others exclaim, "now we can all have applesauce, and apple pie, and apple strudel!" "Provided, of course," so Sylvia rejoins, "that you reduce my labor burden, and/or furnish me with more room in the tent, and/or with more bacon at breakfast." Her claim to (a kind of) ownership of the tree revolts the others.

c. The trippers are walking along a bridle path on which they discover a cache of nuts that some squirrel has abandoned.

Only Leslie, who has been endowed from birth with many knacks and talents, knows how to crack them, but she wants to charge for sharing that information. The campers see no important difference between her demand and Sylvia's.

d. Morgan recognizes the campsite. "Hey, this is where my father camped thirty years ago. This is where he dug a special little pond on the other side of that hill, and stocked it with specially good fish. Dad knew I might come camping here one day, and he did all that so that I could eat better when I'm here. Great. Now I can have better food than you guys have." The rest frown, or smile, at Morgan's greed.

Of course, not everybody likes camping trips. I do not myself enjoy them much, because I'm not outdoorsy, or, at any rate, I'm not outdoorsy overnight-without-a-mattress-wise. There's a limit to the outdoorsiness to which some academics can be expected to submit: I'd rather have my socialism in the warmth of All Souls College than in the wet of the Catskills, and I love modern plumbing. But the question I'm asking is not: wouldn't you like to go on a camping trip? but: isn't this, the socialist way, with collective property and planned mutual giving, rather obviously the *best* way to run a camping trip, whether or not you actually *like* camping?

The circumstances of the camping trip are multiply special: many features distinguish it from the circumstances of life in a modern society. One may therefore not infer, from the fact that camping trips of the sort that I have described are feasible and desirable, that society-wide socialism is equally feasible and equally desirable. There are too many major differences between the contexts for that inference to carry any conviction. What we urgently need to know is precisely *what* are the differences that matter, and how can socialists address them? Because of its contrasts with life in the large, the camping trip model serves well as a reference point for purported demonstrations that socialism across society is not feasible and/or desirable, since it seems eminently feasible and desirable on the trip.

II
THE PRINCIPLES REALIZED ON THE CAMPING TRIP

Two principles are realized on the camping trip, an egalitarian principle, and a principle of community. The community principle constrains the operation of the egalitarian principle by forbidding certain inequalities that the egalitarian principle permits. (The egalitarian principle in question is, as I shall explain, one of radical equality of opportunity: it is therefore consistent with certain inequalities of outcome.)

There are, in fact, a number of potentially competing egalitarian principles with which the camping trip, as I have described it, complies, because the simple circumstances of the trip, unlike more complex ones, do not force a choice among them. But the only egalitarian principle realized on the trip that I shall bring into focus is the one that I regard as the correct egalitarian principle, the egalitarian principle that *justice* endorses, and that is a radical principle of equality of opportunity, which I shall call "socialist equality of opportunity."

Now, equality of opportunity, whether moderate or radical, removes obstacles to opportunity from which some people suffer and others don't, obstacles that are sometimes due to the enhanced opportunities that the more privileged people enjoy. Importantly, the removal of blocks to the opportunity of some people does not always leave the opportunities of the initially better placed intact: sometimes it reduces the opportunities of those who benefit from inequality of opportunity. I underline this point because it means that promoting equality of opportunity is not only an *equalizing*, but also a *redistributing*, policy. Promoting equality of opportunity, in all of its forms, is not merely giving to some what others had and continue to enjoy.

We can distinguish three forms of equality of opportunity and three corresponding obstacles to opportunity: the first form removes one obstacle, the second form removes that one and a second, and the third form removes all three.

First, there is what might be called *bourgeois* equality of opportunity, by which I mean the equality of opportunity that characterizes (at least in aspiration) the liberal age. Bourgeois equality of opportunity removes socially constructed status restrictions, both formal and informal, on life chances. An example of a formal status restriction is that under which a serf labors in a feudal society; an example of an informal status restriction is that from which a person whose skin is the wrong color may suffer in a society that is free of racist law but that nevertheless possesses a racist consciousness that generates racial disadvantage. This first form of equality of opportunity widens people's opportunities by removing constraints on opportunity caused by rights assignments and by bigoted and other prejudicial social perceptions.

Left-liberal equality of opportunity goes beyond bourgeois equality of opportunity. For it also sets itself against the constraining effect of social circumstances by which bourgeois equality of opportunity is undisturbed, the constraining effect, that is, of those circumstances of birth and upbringing that constrain not by assigning an inferior *status* to their victims, but by nevertheless causing them to labor and live under substantial disadvantages. The disadvantage targeted by left-liberal equality of opportunity derives immediately from a person's circumstances and does not depend for its constraining power on social perceptions or on assignments of superior and inferior rights. Policies promoting left-liberal equality of opportunity include head-start education for children from deprived backgrounds. When left-liberal equality of opportunity is fully achieved, people's fates are determined by their native talent and their choices, and, therefore, not at all by their social backgrounds.

Left-liberal equality of opportunity corrects for *social* disadvantage, but not for native, or *inborn*, disadvantage. What I would call *socialist* equality of opportunity treats the inequality that arises out of native differences as a further source of injustice, beyond that imposed by unchosen social backgrounds, since native differences are equally unchosen. (Hence the similarity of the campers' attitudes to Sylvia's good luck and Leslie's, in scenarios b. and c. on pp. 8–9 above.) Socialist equality of opportunity seeks to correct for *all* unchosen disadvantages, disadvantages, that is, for which the agent cannot herself reasonably be held responsible, whether they be disadvantages that reflect social misfortune or disadvantages that reflect natural misfortune. When socialist equality of opportunity prevails, differences of outcome reflect nothing but difference of taste and choice, not differences in natural and social capacities and powers.

So, for example, under socialist equality of opportunity income differences obtain when they reflect nothing but different individual preferences, including income/leisure preferences. People differ in their tastes, not only across consumer items, but also between working only a few hours and consuming rather little on the one hand, and working long hours and consuming rather more on the other. Preferences across income and leisure are not in principle different from preferences across apples and oranges, and there can be no objection to differences in people's benefits and burdens that reflect nothing but different preferences, *when* (which is not always) *their satisfaction leads to a comparable aggregate enjoyment of life*. Such differences in benefits and burdens do not constitute *inequalities* of benefits and burdens.

Let me spell out the analogy at which I have just gestured. A table is before us, laden with apples and oranges. Each of us is entitled to take six pieces of fruit, with apples and oranges appearing in any combination to make up that six. Suppose, now, I complain that Sheila has five

apples whereas I have only three. Then it
should extinguish my sense of grievance,
a sense of grievance that is here totally
inappropriate, when you point out that
Sheila has only one orange whereas I
have three, and that I could have had a
bundle just like Sheila's had I forgone a
couple of oranges. So, similarly, under a
system where each gets the same income
per hour, but can choose how many
hours she works, it is not an intelligible
complaint that some people have more
take-home pay than others. The income/
leisure trade-off is relevantly like the
apples/oranges trade-off: that I have
more income than you do no more
shows, just as such, that we are un-
equally placed than my having four

apples from the table when you have two represents, just as such, an objectionable inequality. (Of course, some people love working, and some hate it, and that could be thought to [and I think it does] induce an injustice in the contemplated scheme, since those who love work will, *ceteris paribus*, relish their lives more than those who hate work do. But the same goes for some people enjoying *each* of apples and oranges more than others do; yet, even so, the apple/orange regime is a giant step toward equality [compared, for example, to a capitalist market society], and so, too, is equal pay for every hour worked, with each choosing the number of hours that she works. Accordingly, and for that reason, and also because this is a short book, I ignore, henceforth, the complication that is exposed within these parentheses. I assume the fulfillment of the condition that was italicized at p. 19 above.)

Now, you might think that I have misused the term "socialist" in the phrase "socialist equality of opportunity," for the simple reason that it is a familiar socialist policy to insist on equality of both income and hours of work: haven't kibbutzim, those paradigms of socialism, worked that way?

I would draw attention, in reply, to the distinction between socialist principles and socialist modes of organization, the first, of course, being the putative justifications of the second. What I call "socialist equality of opportunity" is, as expounded here, a principle, one, so I say, that is satisfied on the camping trip, but I have not said what modes of organization would, and would not, satisfy it in general. And, although the suggested strictly equal work/wage regime would indeed contradict it, I acknowledge that socialists have advocated such regimes, and I have no wish, or need, to deny that those regimes can be called *socialist* work/wage regimes. What I do need to insist is that such systems contradict the fundamental principles animating socialists, when those principles are fully thought through. No defensible fundamental principle of equality or, indeed, of community, taken by itself, warrants such a system, which may nevertheless be amply justified as an appropriate "second best" in light of the constraints of a particular place and time, and also in light of general constraints on the gathering and use of information about the tastes and powers of individuals, and, indeed, on their capacity to supply that information. Although justice might favor sensitivity to how happy or otherwise people are in similar circumstances—see the parenthetical remarks two paragraphs above—it is in general not possible, or even desirable, to fine-tune equality in that way.

What I have called *socialist* equality of opportunity is consistent with three forms of *in*equality, the second and third forms being subtypes of one type. Accordingly, I designate the three forms of inequality as (i), (ii-a), and (ii-b). The first form of inequality is unproblematic, the second form is a bit problematic, and the third is very problematic.

(i) The first type, or form, of inequality is unproblematic because it does not constitute an inequality, all things considered. Variety of preference and choice across lifestyle options means that some people will have more goods of a certain sort than others do, but that is no inequality in the relevant sense, where comparable aggregate enjoyment obtains. That was the lesson of the apples/oranges example, and of its application to income/leisure choices.

(ii) The second type of inequality is problematic, since it does involve an inequality in aggregate benefit. For socialist equality of opportunity tolerates inequality of benefit, where the inequality reflects the genuine choices of parties who are initially equally placed and who may therefore reasonably be held responsible for the consequences of those choices. And this type of inequality takes two forms: inequality that is due to *regrettable choice* and inequality that is due to differences in *option luck*.

(ii-a) To illustrate the first of these forms, imagine that one apple/orange chooser (but not the other) carelessly waits so long that, by the time he picks up the fruit to which he's entitled, it has lost its full savor: the resulting inequality of benefit raises no grievance. And the same goes for someone in a work/pay regime whose ultimate fortune is inferior because she did not bother to examine her job opportunities properly.

These inequalities of aggregate benefit are justified by differential exercises of effort and/or care by people, who are, initially, absolutely equally placed, and who are equal even in their *capacities* to expend effort and care. A stock example is that of the grasshopper and the ant, who must be presumed to be equal in those capacities for the story to carry its customary moral. A mark of the fact that grasshopper/ant presents an inequality of benefit is that the homeless grasshopper retrospectively *regrets* his choice. He does so because he knows that, had he chosen as the ant did, his situation would now be comparable to the ant's, instead of inferior in total benefit (including the benefits of idleness) to that of the ant.

Now you may be a skeptic about the grasshopper/ant story. You may believe (against the grain, I wager, of your reactions to people in ordinary life: see the paragraph that follows) that there is no such thing, ultimately, as being "truly responsible," or "choosing to be idle"; you may believe that greater negligence, for example, can reflect nothing but a smaller capacity for self-application, in the given circumstances, than others have, which should not be penalized. And if that is what you believe, then you will not countenance this second form of inequality. But even if, like me, you are not firmly disposed to disallow it, the question remains, how *large* is this inequality likely to be? Well, that is a very difficult question, and my own view, or hope, is that, under an intelligent institutionalization of the relevant principle, it wouldn't be very large, *on its own*: it can, however, contribute to very high degrees of inequality when it's in synergy with the third and truly problematic form of inequality, that is, ii-b, which is consistent with socialist equality of opportunity.

I said that believing that no inequality could truly reflect real freedom of choice would contradict your reactions to people in day-to-day life, and that I lack that belief. I lack that belief because I am not convinced that it is true *both* that all choices are causally determined *and* that causal determination obliterates responsibility. If you are indeed so convinced, then do not *blame* me for thinking otherwise, do not *blame* right-wing politicians for reducing welfare support (since, in your view, they can't help doing so), do not, indeed, blame, or praise, anyone for choosing to do anything, and therefore live your life, henceforth, differently from the way that we both know that you have lived it up to now.

(ii-b) The truly problematic inequality in overall benefit, the substantial inequality that is consistent with socialist equality of opportunity, is inequality that reflects differences in what philosophers call *option luck*. The paradigm case of option luck is a deliberate gamble. We start out equally placed, with $100 each, and we are relevantly identical in all respects, in character, in talents, and in circumstances. One of the features that we share is a penchant for gambling, so we flip a coin on the understanding that I give you $50 if it comes up heads, and you give me $50 if it comes up tails. I end up with $150 and you end up with $50, and with no extra anythings to offset that monetary shortfall.

This inequality is consistent with socialist equality of opportunity; you and I simply used our radically similar opportunities, and, moreover, in exactly the same way. And unlike the grasshopper, the losing gambler, while of course regretting his loss, need not regret his decision to gamble in the way the grasshopper regrets his decision to be idle. The losing gambler can say: "Faced afresh

31

with the same options, I would have made the same choice; it was a reasonable gamble."

Now this form of inequality does not occur only as a result of gambling narrowly so called. There is also an element of option luck in the generation of market inequalities, which partly reflect gambles about where to put one's money or one's labor. Accordingly, some market-generated inequalities are partly compatible with, and, indeed, partly congruent with, socialist equality of opportunity. But one must not exaggerate the extent to which market inequalities have their genesis in pure market luck: market gambling differs significantly from standard gambling. Standardly, one has a choice whether or not to gamble: gambling is

avoidable. But the market is hardly avoidable in a market society: even the means
of exiting any particular market society
consist of resources that are accessible
only on terms set by that market society.
The market, one might say, is a casino
from which it is difficult to escape, and
the inequalities that it produces are
tainted with injustice for that reason.
Whatever else is true, it is certainly safe
to say that the yawning gulf between rich
and poor in capitalist countries is not
largely due to luck and the lack of it in
optional gambling, but is rather a result
of unavoidable gambling and straightfor-
ward brute luck, where no kind of gambling is involved. To be sure, avoidable
option luck may figure in the explanation
of cases where one entrepreneur prospers

and another fails, but that is not, of course, the sort of inequality that exercises socialists.

Although inequalities of forms (ii-a) and (ii-b) are not condemned by justice, they are nevertheless repugnant to socialists when they obtain on a sufficiently large scale, because they then contradict community: community is put under strain when large inequalities obtain. The sway of socialist equality of opportunity must therefore be tempered by a principle of community, if society is to display the socialist character that makes the camping trip attractive.

"Community" can mean many things, but the requirement of community that is central here is that people care about, and, where necessary and possible, care for, one another, and, too, care that they care about one another. There are two modes of communal caring that I want to discuss here. The first is the mode that curbs some of the inequalities that result from socialist equality of opportunity. The second mode of communal caring is not strictly required for equality, but it is nevertheless of supreme importance in the socialist conception.

We cannot enjoy full community, you and I, if you make, and keep, say, ten times as much money as I do, because my life will then labor under challenges that you will never face, challenges that you could help me to cope with, but do not, because you keep your money. To illustrate. I am rich, and I live an easy life, whereas you are poor, because of regrettable choices and/or bad option luck, and not, therefore because of any lack of equality of opportunity. You have to ride the crowded bus every day, whereas I pass you by in my comfortable car. One day, however, I must take the bus, because my wife needs the car. I can reasonably complain about that to a fellow car-driver, but not to you. I can't say to you: "It's awful that I have to take the bus today." There is a lack of community between us of just the sort that naturally obtains between me and the fellow car-driver. And it will show itself in many other ways, for we enjoy widely different powers to care for ourselves, to protect and care for offspring, to avoid danger, and so on.

I believe that certain inequalities that cannot be forbidden in the name of socialist equality of opportunity should nevertheless be forbidden, in the name of community. But is it an *in*justice to forbid the transactions that generate those inequalities? Do the relevant prohibitions merely define the terms within which justice will operate, or do they sometimes (justifiably?) contradict justice? I do not know the answer to that question. (It would, of course, be a considerable pity if we had to conclude that community and justice were potentially incompatible moral ideals.)

So, to return to the camping trip, suppose that we eat pretty meagerly, but you have your special high-grade fish pond, which you got neither by inheritance nor by chicanery nor as a result of the brute (that is, nonoption) luck of your superior exploratory talent, but as a result of an absolutely innocent option luck that no one can impugn from the point of view of justice: you got it through a lottery that we all entered. Then, even so, even though there is no injustice here, your luck cuts you off from our common life, and the ideal of community condemns that, and therefore also condemns the running of any such lottery.

The other expression of communal caring that is instantiated on the camping trip is a communal form of reciprocity, which contrasts with the market form of reciprocity, as I shall presently explain. Where starting points are equal, and there are independent (of equality of opportunity) limits put on inequality of outcome, then communal reciprocity is not required for equality, but it is nevertheless required for human relationships to take a desirable form.

Communal reciprocity is the antimarket principle according to which I serve you not because of what I can get in return by doing so but because you need or want my service, and you, for the same reason, serve me. Communal reciprocity is not the same thing as market reciprocity, since the market motivates productive contribution not on the basis of commitment to one's fellow human beings and a desire to serve them while being served *by* them, but on the basis of cash reward. The immediate motive to productive ac-

tivity in a market society is (not always
but) typically some mixture of greed and
fear, in proportions that vary with the
details of a person's market position and
personal character. It is true that people
can engage in market activity under other
inspirations, but the motives of greed
and fear are what the market brings to
prominence, and that includes greed on
behalf of, and fear for the safety of, one's
family. Even when one's concerns are
thus wider than those of one's mere self,
the market posture is greedy and fearful
in that one's opposite-number marketeers
are predominantly seen as possible
sources of enrichment, and as threats to
one's success. These are horrible ways of
seeing other people, however much we
have become habituated and inured to

them, as a result of centuries of capitalist civilization. (Capitalism did not, of course, invent greed and fear: they are deep in human nature. But, unlike its predecessor feudal civilization, which had the [Christian or other] grace to condemn greed, capitalism celebrates it.)

I said that, within communal reciprocity, I produce in a spirit of commitment to my fellow human beings: I desire to serve them while being served by them, and I get satisfaction from each side of that equation. In such motivation, there is indeed an expectation of reciprocation, but it differs critically from the reciprocation expected in market motivation. If I am a marketeer, then I am willing to serve, but only in order to *be* served: I would not serve if doing so were not a means to get service. Accordingly, I give as little service as I can in exchange for as much service as I can get: I want to buy cheap and sell dear. I serve others *either* in order to get something that I desire—that is the greed motivation; *or* in order to ensure that something that I seek to avoid is avoided—that is the fear motivation. A marketeer, considered just as such, does not value cooperation with others for its own sake: she does not value the conjunction, *serve-and-be-served*, as such.

A nonmarket cooperator relishes cooperation itself: what I want, as a nonmarketeer, is that we serve each other; and when I serve, instead of trying to get whatever I can get, I do not regard my action as, all things considered, a sacrifice. To be sure, I serve you in the expectation that (if you are able to) you will also serve me. My commitment to socialist community does not require me to be a sucker who serves you regardless of whether (if you are able to do so) you are going to serve me, but I nevertheless find value in both parts of the conjunction—I serve you *and* you serve me—and in that conjunction itself: I do not regard the first part—I serve you—as simply a means to my real end, which is that you serve me. The relationship between us under communal reciprocity is not the market-instrumental one in which I give because I get, but the noninstrumental one in which I give because you need, or want, and in which I expect a comparable generosity from you.

For ease and vividness of exposition, I characterized communal reciprocity in the foregoing paragraphs in two-person (I-you) terms. But communal reciprocity can link chains of people no pair of whom directly give to one another: in a spirit of communal reciprocity that encompasses us all, I can serve you and you her and she him and he me. Communal networks that are in some ways structurally like market networks can form, under a different animating motivation. They are like them only in some ways because in a market network no one does anything for anyone without getting something from *that* person.

Because motivation in market exchange consists largely of greed and fear, a person typically does not care *fundamen-*

tally, within market interaction, about how well or badly anyone other than herself fares. You cooperate with other people not because you believe that cooperating with other people is a good thing in itself, not because you want yourself *and* the other person to flourish, but because *you* seek to gain and you know that you can do so only if you cooperate with others. In every type of society people perforce provision one another: a society *is* a network of mutual provision. But, in market society, that mutuality is only a by-product of an unmutual and fundamentally *non*reciprocating attitude.

III
IS THE IDEAL DESIRABLE?

It is the aspiration of socialists to realize
the principles that structure life on the
camping trip on a national, or even on an
international, scale. Socialists therefore
face two distinct questions, which are
often not treated as distinctly as they
should be. The first is: would socialism, if
feasible, be desirable? The second is: is socialism feasible?

Some might say that the camping trip
is itself unattractive, that, as a matter of
principle, there should be *scope* for much
greater inequality and instrumental treatment of other people, even in small-scale
interaction, than the ethos of the camping

trip permits. These opponents of the camping trip ethos would not, of course, recommend society-wide equality and community *as* extensions to the large of what is desirable in the small, and they are unlikely to recommend for the large what they disparage even in the small.

The opponents in question do not say that there *should* be more inequality and treating of people as mere means on a camping trip, but just that people have a *right* to make personal choices, even if the result is inequality and/or instrumental treatment of people, and, so they say, that right is not honored on the camping trip. But this criticism seems to me to be misplaced. For there *is* a right to personal choice on the camping trip, and there are plenty of private choices on it, in leisure,

and in labor (where there is more than
one reasonable way of distributing it),
under the voluntarily accepted constraint
that those choices must blend fairly with
the personal choices of others. Within
market society, too, the choices of others
massively confine each individual's pursuit of her own choices, but that fact is
masked in market society, because, unlike
what's true on the camping trip, in market society the unavoidable mutual depen-
dence of human beings is not brought
into common consciousness, as a datum
for formal and informal planning. A particular person in a market society may
face a choice of being a building laborer
or a carer or starving, his set of choices
being a consequence of everybody else's
choices. But nobody designed things that

way, and his restricted options consequently misappear as mere facts of life.

Although few would take the line that
I have just opposed, which says that it is
all right for camping trips *themselves* to be
run on market lines, many would point
to features special to the camping trip
that distinguish it from the normal mill of
life in a modern society and that consequently cast doubt on the desirability
and/or the feasibility of realizing camping trip principles in such a society. Such
people might grant that I have displayed
the attractiveness, and the feasibility, of
socialist values, but only in the course of
a substantially recreational activity, in
which there are no competing social
groups, in which everyone to whom you
relate is known to you personally and

observed by you daily, and in which an individual's family ties exert no counter-pull to his sense of social obligation. To what extent do these differences render the ideal un-, or less, desirable? And to what extent do they render it, im-, or less, practicable?

I do not see that the stated differences undermine the desirability of the spread across society of camping trip values. I do not think that the cooperation and un-selfishness that the trip displays are ap-propriate only among friends, or within a small community. In the mutual provi-sioning of a market society, I am essen-tially indifferent to the fate of the farmer whose food I eat: there is no or little com-munity between us, as that value was ar-ticulated in Part II above. In the next Part

I address the question whether it is feasible to proceed otherwise. But it does seem to me that all people of goodwill would welcome the news that it had become possible to proceed otherwise, perhaps, for example, because some economists had invented clever ways of harnessing and organizing our capacity for generosity to others. I continue to find appealing the sentiment of a left-wing song that I learned in my childhood, which begins as follows: "If we should consider each other, a neighbor, a friend, or a brother, it could be a wonderful, wonderful world, it could be a wonderful world." The point is often made, in resistance to the sentiment of the song, that one cannot be friends with the millions of people who compose a large society: that idea is at best impossible to realize, and, so some add, it is even incoherent, because of the exclusivity that goes with friendship. But the song need not be interpreted in that overambitious fashion. It suffices that I treat everyone with whom I have any exchange or other form of contact as someone toward whom I have the reciprocating attitude that is characteristic of friendship. And general social friendship, that is, community, is, like friendship, not an all-or-nothing thing. It is surely a welcome thing when more rather than less community is present in society.

But whatever we may wish to conclude about the *desirability* of socialism, we must also address the independent question of its *feasibility*, to which I now turn.

IV

IS THE IDEAL FEASIBLE?
ARE THE OBSTACLES TO IT
HUMAN SELFISHNESS, OR
POOR SOCIAL TECHNOLOGY?

Whether or not the socialist relations of the camping trip are attractive, and whether or not it would also be desirable for such relations to spread across society as a whole, many people who have thought about the matter have judged socialism to be *infeasible* for society as a whole. "Socialism in one short camping trip, maybe. But socialism across society, all the time? You gotta be kidding! The camping trip is a happy recreational context, in which people are removed from the complexity of everyday life and willing to suspend their normal operating principles. It is almost *by definition* special. Nothing in it reduces the implausibility of the idea of socialism on a grand scale."

It is worth pointing out, to begin with, that it is not only in happy contexts, but also in much less benign ones, that camping trip attitudes tend to prevail. People regularly participate in emergencies like flood or fire on camping trip principles. But let us look at the question about the feasibility of socialism more closely.

There are two contrasting reasons why society-wide socialism might be thought infeasible, and it is very important, both intellectually and politically, to distin-

guish them. The first reason has to do
with the limits of human nature, and the
second has to do with the limits of social
technology. The first putative reason why
socialism is infeasible is that people are,
so it is often said, by nature insufficiently
generous and cooperative to meet its re-
quirements, however generous and cooperative they may be within the frame of
limited time and special intimacy in
which the camping trip unrolls. The
second putative reason why socialism is
infeasible is that, even *if* people are, or
could become, in the right culture, sufficiently generous, we do not know how
to harness that generosity; we do not
know how, through appropriate rules
and stimuli, to make generosity turn the
wheels of the economy. Contrast human

selfishness, which we know how to harness very well.

Of course, even if neither of these problems, and no comparable ones, obtained, socialism might still be unattainable, because political and ideological forces— including the enormous practical force of the belief that socialism is infeasible— that would resist a movement toward socialism are too strong. But the question about feasibility that I am addressing here is *not* whether socialism is straightforwardly *accessible*, whether we can get to it from where we are, and burdened as we are with a massive legacy of capitalism and with all the other contingencies that compose our current social condition. The present feasibility question is about whether socialism would work, and be stable, if we were indeed in a position to institute it. And an important aspect of that question is whether the working of a socialist society would reinforce, or, rather, undermine, the communal and egalitarian preferences that are required for socialism's stability. (We must, moreover, also ask a question that I shall not pursue here, which is whether socialism is consistent not only with the springs of human nature but also with human nature as it has been shaped by capitalism; the forces that might block the installation of socialism might also operate so as to foil its efficient working.)

In my view, the principal problem that faces the socialist ideal is that we do not know how to design the machinery that would make it run. Our problem is not,

primarily, human selfishness, but our lack
of a suitable organizational technology:
our problem is a problem of *design*. It
may be an *insoluble* design problem, and
it is a design problem that is undoubtedly
exacerbated by our selfish propensities,
but a design problem, so I think, is what
we've got.

Both selfish and generous propensities
reside, after all, in (almost?) everyone.
Our problem is that, while we know how
to make an economic system work on the
basis of the development, and, indeed,
the hypertrophy, of selfishness, we do not
know how to make it work by devel-
oping and exploiting human generosity.
Yet even in the real world, in our own society, a great deal depends on generosity,

or, to put it more generally and more negatively, on nonmarket incentives. Doctors, nurses, teachers and others do not, or do not comprehensively, gauge what they do in their jobs according to the amount of money they're likely to get as a result, in the way that capitalists and workers in noncaring occupations do. (The aforementioned carers won't, of course, work for nothing, but that is like the fact that you need to eat on the camping trip: it does not follow, and it is false, that carers tailor their work to expected monetary return.) And the reason for the difference is not that carers are made of morally superior clay, but, in good part, the more cognitive reason that their conception of what is to be produced is guided by a conception of human need: market signals are not necessary to decide what diseases to cure or what subjects to teach, nor are they efficient means of deciding that. But, once we pass out of the sphere of need, or, more generally, of goods that everyone can be expected to want, to the wide sphere of optional commodities, and we pass increasingly to that as economies progress and as life therefore becomes easier and more elegant, it also becomes more difficult to know what to produce, and how to produce it, without the device of market signals: very few socialist economists would now dissent from that proposition. One reason why the camping trip can readily do without market exchange is that the information that the campers need to plan their activities is modest in extent, and comparatively easy to obtain and to aggregate.

Now, market prices serve two logically distinguishable functions: an *information* function and a *motivation* function. First, they make known how much people would be willing to sacrifice to obtain given goods and services: they show how valuable goods are to people, and thereby reveal what is worth producing. But, distinctly, market prices serve as a motivation to provide people with the goods in question: the marketeer seeks to capture, for her own gain, what people are prepared to pay. The two functions are not only logically separable: sometimes the first operates without the second, as when an official who acts, for example, on behalf of a charity, seeks to maximize the revenue from its endowment, but transparently not in order to line her own pockets: she does not keep the money that accrues, and, at least in certain cases, her own income is unaffected by how well the fund she manages performs.

In the light of the infirmities of comprehensive planning on the one hand and of the injustice of market results and the moral shabbiness of market motivation on the other, it is natural to ask whether it might be practically feasible to preserve the information function of the market, to continue to get the benefits it provides of information generation and processing with respect to what should be produced, while extinguishing its normal motivational presuppositions and distributive consequences. Can we have market efficiency in production without market incentives, and, hence, without a market distribution of rewards?

Precisely that distinction is the center of a groundbreaking book by Joseph Carens, who works in the Political Science Department at the University of Toronto. The book, published by the University of Chicago Press in 1981, was called *Equality, Moral Incentives, and the Market*, and its significant subtitle was *An Essay in Utopian Politico-Economic Theory*. Carens described a society in which what looks like a standard capitalist market organizes economic activity, but the tax system cancels the disequalizing results of that market by redistributing income to complete equality. There are (pretax) profit-seeking capitalists, and workers who own no capital, *but* people acknowledge an obligation to serve others, and the extent to which they discharge that obligation is measured by how close their pretax income is to what it would be in the most remunerative (and therefore, on standard assumptions, the most socially contributing) activity available to them, while taxation effects a fully egalitarian posttax distribution of income. Here, then, producers aim, in an immediate sense, at cash results, but they do not keep (or otherwise benefit from) the money that accrues, and they seek it out of a desire to contribute to society: a market mechanism is used to solve the social technology problem, in the service of equality and community.

There are plenty of problems with the Carens scheme, but it seems to me to be one that is amply worth refining, and the principle of the scheme enjoys a modest measure of realization whenever better-off people do not decide to reduce their labor input in the face of adverse redistributive taxation because they approve of the purpose to which the taxation is put.

The Carens scheme is Utopian partly in that it relies entirely on non-self-interested choice. But there are ways of introducing strong elements of community and equality into an economic system in which self-interested choice nevertheless continues to obtain, but now with confined scope. One familiar such way is through the institution of a welfare state, which takes a great deal of provision for need out of the market system. A less familiar way is through the institution of *market* socialism, on which more in a moment. Each of these systems works only if people are unself-interested *enough* to accept the constraints that the systems put on the pursuit of self-interest.

Whereas many socialists have recently put their faith in market socialism, nineteenth-century socialists were, by contrast, for the most part opposed to market organization of economic life. The mainstream socialist pioneers favored something that they thought would be far superior, to wit, comprehensive central planning, which, it was hoped, could realize the socialist ideal of a truly sharing society. And the pioneers' successors were encouraged by what they interpreted as victories of planning, such as the industrialization of the Soviet Union and the early institution of educational and medical provision in the People's Republic of China. But central planning, at least as practiced in the past, is, we now know, a poor recipe for economic success, at any rate once a society has provided itself with the essentials of a modern productive system.

Now, since, historically, the idea of socialism was strongly linked to that of central planning, economists of socialist persuasion did not, until recently, study noncentral planning ways of organizing what would remain in one key respect a socialist economy, in that the assets used to produce things are shared. Market socialism is called "socialist" because it abolishes the division between capital and labor: there is, in market socialism, no class of capitalists facing workers who own no capital, since workers themselves, that is, the whole population, own the capital of firms (though not necessarily of the very firms that they work in, as will be illustrated two paragraphs on). Economic inequality is thereby substantially diminished. And there now exist various designs for workers' ownership, for different forms of semipublic ownership, for example, at a municipal level, and other attempts to formulate a realization of the principle of collective ownership in the absence of central state direction of all economic activity.

Market socialism is, however, unlike traditionally conceived socialism in that its worker or publicly owned firms confront one another, and consumers, in market-competitive fashion; and market socialism is also, and relatedly, unlike traditionally conceived socialism in that it reduces, even though it does not entirely eliminate, the traditional socialist emphasis on economic equality. Equality is prejudiced because market competition leads to inequality between winners and losers. And community, too, is prejudiced, under market socialism, because exchange under market socialism is no less market exchange than it is under capitalism: it is not, as it is in the Carensian economy described above, only superficially market exchange. True reciprocity, express rather than merely implicit reciprocity (see pp. pp. 39–45 above), does not prevail, at the heart of market socialism's economic transactions. But it lies in the background of the system: the values of equality and reciprocity justify the constraints under which the socialist market functions, and all of that is true, too, of the welfare state, and of the proposal that the state ensure that all of its citizens have a substantial market-independent *basic income.*

A particularly careful design of market socialism can be found in the book *A Future for Socialism,* by the Yale economist John Roemer, which was published in 1994 by Harvard University Press. In Roemer's scheme, each citizen enjoys a birthright entitlement to a per capita share of her country's total capital assets. She is free to trade the vouchers that represent her share on the stock market, and thereby, with skill and luck, to obtain more stock and/or more dividend income than others, but she may not realize her stock so as to convert it into such goods as mansions, yachts, Dior gowns, and so forth: shares in firms are inconvertible into ordinary money, nor can they be bought with ordinary money, but only with other shares. And, on her demise, a person's shares return to the treasury so that new birthrights to capital assets can be formed. The labor market, on the other hand, is not otherwise changed, so its inequalities remain, but not, now, in inflating synergy with the capital/labor divide.

In brief, the system is like a traditional capitalist market economy except that one market is closed: the one on which exchanges can be made of firm stock for money that buys consumption goods. The capitalist class is liquidated, but the efficiency results of the capitalist market are, Roemer claims, achieved, by different means.

To illustrate the latter point. Large shareholders in given firms standardly discipline those firms into efficient operation in a capitalist economy: their shares are large enough for them to have an immediate and substantial stake in how well the firm functions. But in Roemer's market socialism the dynamic of stock transactions will spread each individual's portfolio across many firms, with no individual having enough stock, or, therefore, stake, in any given firm, to undertake the required disciplining role. That role is therefore assigned to banks and other financial institutions, as prefigured by what actually now happens in the Japanese *Keiretsu* system, and in Germany.

Being an economist, Roemer is concerned to show that his system is not less efficient than capitalism. But suppose he is wrong. Suppose his scheme, or any comparable socialist or semisocialist scheme, is somewhat less efficient than standard capitalism. The right inference from that need not be that we should keep capitalism: efficiency is, after all, only one value, and it would show a lack of balance to insist that even small deficits in that value should be eliminated at whatever cost to the values of equality and community. For efficiency, in the relevant sense, only means providing the goods and services that you want when you do not take into account (other aspects of) the quality of your life, and the quality of your relations to your fellow citizens. Why should we make *no* sacrifice of the former for the sake of the latter?

Market socialism does not fully satisfy socialist standards of distributive justice, but it scores far better by those standards than market capitalism does, and is therefore an eminently worthwhile project, from a socialist point of view. Market socialism nevertheless remains deficient from that point of view, because, by socialist standards, there is injustice in a system that confers high rewards on people who happen to be unusually talented and who form highly productive cooperatives. Market socialism is also a deficient socialism because the market exchange that lies at its heart tends against the value of community.

But could we go further than Roemer in a nonmarket direction? I do not know whether the needed refinements are possible, nor do I know, speaking more generally, whether the full socialist ideal is feasible, in the Carensian, or in some other form. We socialists don't *now* know how to replicate camping trip procedures on a nationwide scale, amid the complexity and variety that comes with nationwide size. We don't *now* know how to give collective ownership and equality the real meaning that it has in the camping trip story but which it didn't have in the Soviet Union and in similarly ordered states. The camping trip's confined temporal, spatial, and population scale mean that, within its confines, the right to personal choice can be exercised, without strain, consistently with equality and community. But while that can happen in the small, we do not know how to honor personal choice, consistently with equality and community, on a large social scale. But I do not think that we now know that we will never know how to do these things: I am agnostic on that score.

The technology for using base motives to productive economic effect is reasonably well understood. Indeed, the history of the twentieth century encourages the thought that the easiest way to generate productivity in a modern society is by nourishing the motives of which I spoke earlier, namely, those of greed and fear. But we should never forget that greed and fear are repugnant motives. Who would propose running a society on the basis of such motives, and thereby promoting the psychology to which they belong, if they were not known to be effective, if they did not have the instrumental value which is the only value that they have? In the famous statement in which Adam Smith justified market relations, he pointed out that we place our faith not in the butcher's generosity but in his self-interest when we rely on him to provision us. Smith thereby propounded a wholly instrumental justification of market motivation, in face of what he acknowledged to be its unattractive intrinsic character. Old-style socialists often

ignore Smith's point, in a moralistic con-
demnation of market motivation that fails
to address its instrumental justification.
Certain contemporary overenthusiastic
market socialists tend, contrariwise, to
forget that the market is intrinsically
repugnant, because they are blinded by
their belated discovery of the market's
instrumental value. It is the genius of the
market that it (1) recruits low-grade
motives to (2) desirable ends; but (3) it
also produces undesirable effects, including significant unjust inequality. In a
balanced view, all three sides of that proposition must be kept in focus, but many
market socialists now self-deceptively
overlook (1) and (3). Both (1) and (2)
were kept in focus by the pioneering

eighteenth-century writer Bernard Mande-
ville, whose market-praising *Fable of the
Bees* was subtitled *Private Vices, Public
Benefits*. Many contemporary celebrants
of the market play down the truth in the
first part of that subtitle.

V
CODA

Any attempt to realize the socialist ideal runs up against entrenched capitalist power and individual human selfishness. Politically serious people must take those obstacles seriously. But they are not reasons to disparage the ideal itself. Disparaging the ideal because it faces those obstacles leads to confusion, and confusion generates disoriented practice: there are contexts where the ideal *can* be advanced, but is pushed forward less resolutely than it might be, because of a lack of clarity about what the ideal is.

The socialist aspiration is to extend community and justice to the whole of

our economic life. As I have acknowledged, we now know that we do not now
know how to do that, and many think
that we now know that it is impossible to
do that. But community conquests in
certain domains, such as health care and
education, have sustained viable forms of
production and distribution in the past,
and it is imperative, now, to defend community, since it is a value that is currently
under aggressive threat from the market
principle. The natural tendency of the
market is to increase the scope of the social relations that it covers, because entre-
preneurs see opportunities at the edge to
turn what is not yet a commodity into
one. Left to itself, the capitalist dynamic
is self-sustaining, and socialists therefore
need the power of organized politics to

oppose it: their capitalist opponents, who go with the grain of the system, need that power less (which is not to say that they lack it!).

I agree with Albert Einstein that socialism is humanity's attempt "to overcome and advance beyond the predatory phase of human development." Every market, even a socialist market, is a system of predation. Our attempt to get beyond predation has thus far failed. I do not think the right conclusion is to give up.

ACKNOWLEDGMENT

A version of this essay was previously published in *Democratic Equality: What Went Wrong?*, edited by Edward Broadbent (University of Toronto Press, 2001).